Copyright © 2019 Orna Ross
The author's's moral rights have been asserted.
All rights reserved.

Font Publications is the publishing imprint for Orna Ross's fiction and poetry, the Go Creative! books and planners and Alliance of Independent Authors publishing guides.

All Enquiries: sarah@ornaross.com

NIGHT LIGHT AS IT RISES
Inspirational Poetry for Bereavement & Other Hard Times
E-book: 978-1-913588-95-3
Paperback: 978-1-913588-96-0
Large Print: 978-1-913588-97-7
Hardback: 978-1-913588-98-4
Audiobook: 978-1-913588-99-1

NIGHT LIGHT AS IT RISES

INSPIRATIONAL POETRY FOR BEREAVEMENT &
OTHER HARD TIMES

TWELVE POEMS TO INSPIRE
BOOK TWO

ORNA ROSS

CONTENTS

Twelve Poems to Inspire Series   xi

NIGHTLIGHT AS IT RISES

Part I
ACCEPT
Dark Night	5
Raindrop Spray	8
Anne's Tree	11
Unfurling	15

Part II
ALIGHT
Brightness of Brightness	21
The Hour Before Dawn	25
Long Light	29
Nightlight As It Rises	32

Part III
ALLOW
Samsara	37
Above the Water Line	41
Last Promise	44
Passing On	48

Let's Keep in Touch	53
Award Winning Inspirational Poetry	55
Acknowledgments	59
About The Poet	61

For my father, Con, in memory

"Grief is the price we pay for love."

— *QUEEN ELIZABETH II OF ENGLAND*

TWELVE POEMS TO INSPIRE SERIES

Nightlight As It Rises is the second book in the *Twelve Poems to Inspire* series, poetry gift books for every occasion.

Each poem is illustrated with a picture or photograph from a contemporary artist and makes a beautiful gift for yourself or a loved one.

Inspirational poetry, as I write it, is not all jolly positivity. Spirit, the source of inspiration, moves in mystery. You will find a variety of moods in these poems and pictures but all are intended to be inspirational in the widest and deepest sense—to uplift and intensify our experience of life.

It takes a great reader to make a great poem. Thank you for reading and sharing inspirational poetry.

x Orna

NIGHTLIGHT AS IT RISES

POEMS TO INSPIRE: BOOK II

PART I
ACCEPT

DARK NIGHT

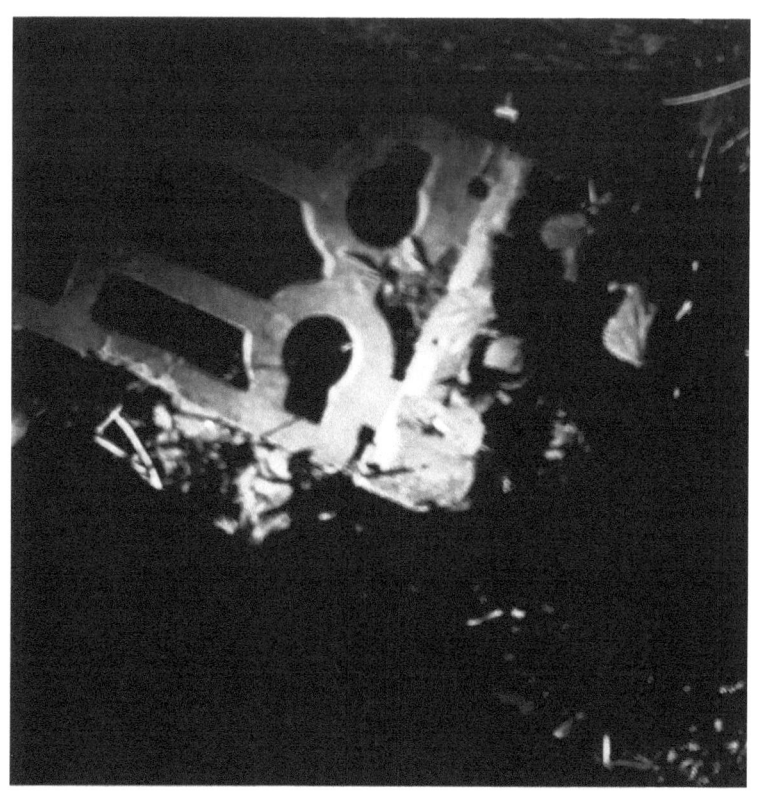

"Suffer the silence. Let all rest in naught." Image: Orna Ross

DARK NIGHT

Life said to the wanderer
Wait without waiting. Kneel
yourself down there, on
stone-hearted stone.

Set down your hope too.
It could be mistaken. And
fold up your map. It
may also be wrong.

Though it be dark here
Beyond all believing, with
no place for faith, no,
just rock-hardened rock,

unfasten, for now, the great
weight of your seeking — it
may, as you say, someday
be your return. But

not even love is
by you here needed. Suffer
the silence. Let
all rest in naught.

Stay down, if you can,
eyes blind and knees bleeding.
All lost, all forsaken,
unready for thought.

RAINDROP SPRAY

"Look at that spray of raindrops...the way it holds the sun..." Image: Jane Dixon-Smith

THAT SPRAY OF RAINDROPS

"Look," she starts to say.
"Look at that spray of raindrops
on that pink petal there,
the way it holds the sun…"
and then recalls that he, the only one
who ever saw such things the same,
will never see such things again.
He's gone.

And nothing for it now
but hold in place
while outraged heart again
beats out its beats of pain.
He's gone. He's gone.
To gaze, as he would have gazed,
and there remain,
until the drops of rain
and the petals glistening
in the sun can be felt again
as one, and she can go on.

ANNE'S TREE

"... can you somehow see your young tree, stretching towards what it can be?"
Image: Aaron Burdon

ANNE'S TREE

I

Our Anne.
We watched her freeze
from root to peak.
It took years.
Began at her feet
moved up through her calves,
then her knees,
set her sitting in a chair
that had wheels,
knocked her flat on her back
ferocious indifferent disease.

Anne.
More than the mind
that railed in her head,
more than the body
betrayed in her bed,
more than the name
that found itself wailed,
as Anne, our great lady,
was felled.

II

Afterwards, Anne, thanks to your niece,
we planted a tree, a plaque underneath.
Three winters on, its grown strong
thickened its twigs, laid in more leaves.
The day it was planted, your nephew
read a poem about you, the first he released.

Now your young tree stretches towards
what it will be. Though its fullness
may take four hundred years
it was there from the seed:
the joyful extent of its reach.

An oak, king of trees: no less
would do. Oh yes, you loved the best
and knew so well when to give,
and what can't be saved.
Your plaque will always read:
Generous. Fun-loving. Brave.

UNFURLING

"...unfurling long ribbons of white..." Image: Daniel Norris

UNFURLING

And now the wave
he is watching
is breaking, breaking, breaking,
unfurling long ribbons
of white along the shore
while out on the quiet horizon
only a shade separates
black sky from black sea.

Last time he saw the ocean,
he was twelve. Then too
he almost missed it,
both sky and sea that day
were the color of jeans.

When he has a mind to,
he can half-be that child,
who used to stoop over a scissors
in his mother's sewing room,
cutting the bottom rungs
off old denim legs.

Who has he become, now,
coming out here, try to see
where air turns to water?
He knows that clouds deliver rain,
that seasons open and close. Why
circle the bewildering waves?

His segment of earth
is sliding toward night,

dropping its asymmetrical self
away from the unraveling sun,
trailing a thread of light
across a blackening horizon
searching to see if the moon
might find its face.

PART II
ALIGHT

BRIGHTNESS OF BRIGHTNESS

"I fled your light, o brightness of brightness..." Image by Ilja Tulit

BRIGHTNESS OF BRIGHTNESS

This is an adaptation of a famous old Irish poem "Gile na Gile" (Brightness of Brightness) written in Gaelic by an 18th century Irish poet, Aodhagán Ó Rathaille, and translated into English by many, including Padraig Pearse, one of the executed signatories of the 1916 Irish Proclamation. The original was an aisling poem, lamenting Ireland's dispossession. Pearse subverted its passive sorrow into a poem of renunciation and revolution. My version is about the renunciation of love, more generally.

> I saw you naked,
> O beauty of beauty,
> covered my eyes.
> Averted my fall.
>
> I closed my mind
> O dreamer of dreamings,
> hardened my thinking
> for fear of my fall.
>
> I tasted your mouth,
> O sweetness of sweetness,
> pulled myself loose
> away from my fall.
>
> I heard your keening
> O sorrow of sorrows,
> hands to my ears.
> I turned from my fall.

I fled your light
O brightness of brightness.
Forever I walk now
recalling my fall.

THE HOUR BEFORE DAWN

"...*the tide of night rest, or restlessness, on the ebb* ..." Image by Jeremy Bishop

THE HOUR BEFORE DAWN

In the hour before dawn, water is first
to hint towards light's returning.
The black pond silvers, and out to sea,
a line of orange begins to crayon
the underlip of the sky.

In the hour before dawn,
gulls untuck their beaks, and take off,
screaming new-day news at the waves.
Inland, along branches and twigs,
thrushes and blackbirds awaken their singing.
Under roofs, humans stir and stretch,
the tide of night rest, or restlessness,
on the ebb. Early risers rise, listen in to devices,
or join the wrens and warblers in whistle and song.

In the hour before dawn, as the sun
starts to layer the air with colours of fire,
sparrows and finches add their voices,
our neighbours' electric light show that flashes
all through the night—red and blue
on and off, blue and red off and on—
turns itself off. Off now for hours to come,
heralding the moment is about to arrive.

Our eyes turn towards it,
though we know it is the earth,
not the sun, that is moving,
we seek the illusion of gravity defied,
of the great star seeming to rise,

flooding our part of the planet with light,
as we once again find ourselves borne
to the end of the hour before dawn.

LONG LIGHT

"...feet that carried her everywhere, once..." Image: Susan Schuster

LONG LIGHT

Every light creates a shadow,
the stars can't shine without the night.
Seek to muffle up your sorrow:
feel life fade inside and out.
Loose it. Let it sear you hollow,
prise you open, clear your throat.
Long light lives by grace of shadow.
The stars are pleased to shine through night.

NIGHTLIGHT AS IT RISES

"...the blessing of the great rains ." Image: AI generated via Sudowrite

NIGHTLIGHT AS IT RISES

May the blessing of the soft rains
be on your house.
May they water your garden,
seeping into your clay
that flowers might spring,
and shed sweetness on the air.

May the blessing of the great rains
be on your house.
May they beat upon your door,
washing it clear
as the ceiling of the sky after a storm,
is erased of fear.

May the blessings of all rains
leave many a pool around your house,
where the blue of heaven can shine,
and the black night float its darkness,
and sometimes too its stars.

And may daylight as it falls,
and nightlight as it rises
find you gentle with each other,
outside your house, and in.

PART III
ALLOW

SAMSARA

"...parts of me have always been free. Composed of wide oceans and many galaxies..." Image: Pawel Nolbert

SAMSARA

> *For my zen and poetic master, Thich Nhat Hanh,*
> *who gave me some of these words and this understanding*
> *when I most needed it.*

If I am not to be flung into chaos,
If I am not to be scattered
in the whirlpool of grief,
if my days are to continue to count,
you must know something:
I have not become nothing.

Things are forever forming
and reforming,
taking on new incarnations.
It is not possible for a thing
to turn into nothing.

Nothing is contained within everything,
every atom, every star, every cell.
Everything is contained within nothing.

This is not a matter of belief.
This is science, a matter of matter.
This is the story of life on earth.

My body was never all of me.
Part of me has always been free,
composed of wide oceans
and many galaxies.
And we were always changing,
you and me.

My death, like my birth,
was an opening, allowing
a slip of my immensity through.

So now: smile to me, sing to me,
call me by my name, in our old easy way.
Wherever you go, now, let me be there.
Present, forever, in you.

ABOVE THE WATER LINE

"...all for want of knowing that other self, that always welled...inside..." Image: Callie Street

Lipstick perfected,
in a water dress, she sighs
for how he made her feel.
His slender, searching tongue
his well-honed, gripping thighs.

The sight of her best self
revealed, shining in his eyes.

Whatever happens to her next,
he happened then, and now
she lies, hot-held, skin-peeled
vitrified. Half naked
in a murky bath,
afraid to stay alive.

And all for want of knowing
that other self that always welled,
concealed from her, inside.

It's holding her afloat, right now,
above the water line.

LAST PROMISE

"...The wood protects us. It cannot bear for us to see it all. We are too small." *Image: K. Mitch Hodge*

LAST PROMISE

Promise me,
that when the leaves turn
in the wind or in the falling,
you'll remember. And smile
at this day spent
under the green ocean dome
that welled above us,
each leaf-flutter a quark
of forest time shifting
and regrouping,

but yet the whole
—the copse within the wood
that is the whole of it to us—
set slow. Slower, the further out
we look, to where our eyes
could only see an army-band
of trunks upholding stillness.

The wood protects us.
It cannot bear for us to see it all.
We are too small.

So when the coming time is here
and you see a leaf is turning
green to brown, beginning its intention
to descend, anticipating the day
of its great fall, twisting,
pirouetting almost
high above the forest floor
that's calling: come.

When you see it twist
this way, then that,
testing the stick of its stalk,
the heft of its trust, look.

Look closer, past the color
of its sap,
the flow of its line
in space, in time,
and know that it has practiced
what it needs, all summer long,
dancing with the wind.

And think of me
and how I loved the leaves
and brought you here
to see you smile.

And smile.
Now, promise me.

PASSING ON

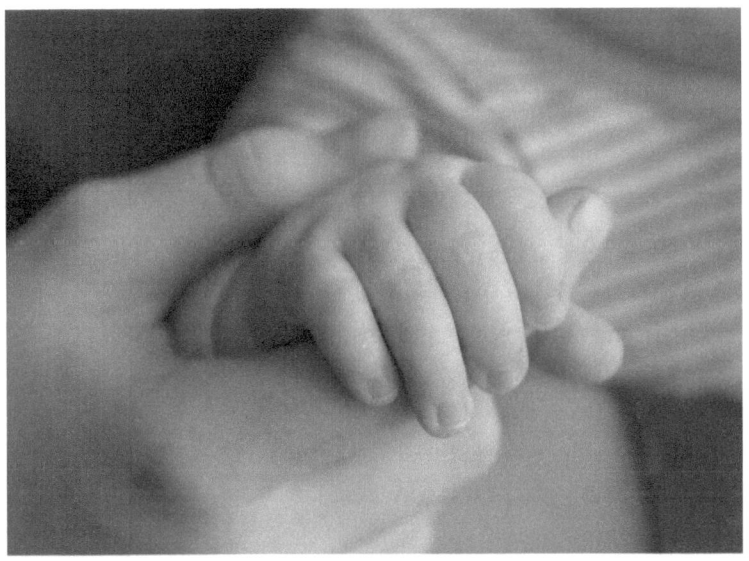

"...when you yearn for our times gone, lay soft hands upon someone." Image: Diana Polekhina

Dear one whom I have loved,
it's here: my time has run,
my breath and flesh have come undone,
and left behind these words
to thank you, from beyond,
for all that you have been
and to remind you of this truth:
I am not gone.

Look for me in my children;
in those who understood my work;
the friends I've known and loved;
my family of birth, where for me it all began.

And the older origin: the seas and trees,
who'll bring you news from here,
where I now am.

And if you find you need to cry
I ask that when you do,
you cry with all the others
passing through, beside you,
along the street of need.

And when you yearn for our times gone,
lay soft hands upon someone.
Give then to them what,
in that hour, you long
to give to me.

Now all that's left of me
is love, pass love along so that
I may live on.

LET'S KEEP IN TOUCH

Enjoyed the poems? Would you like more? If you're online, we have lots of ways to continue the poetic conversation.

UPDATES & BONUSES

I write a new poem every few days and love sharing inspirations and ideas with my poetry pen-friends. My monthly email will bring you my inspirational poetry news and ideas, discounted books, and other pen-friend presents. Follow the link below to become my poetry pen-friend and get a **free e-book**:

OrnaRoss.com/Free-Poetry

PLEASE REVIEW THIS BOOK ONLINE

If you enjoyed this book, please give it a quick review online by visiting the link below and selecting the "Reviews" tab. Your review doesn't have to be long or detailed. A quick star rating and a sentence or two that helps others to understand the value of this book is all that's needed. I appreciate the support more than you know. *Go raibh maith agat!*

OrnaRoss.comNightLightAsItRises

BECOME A PATRON

I reserve exclusive poems, special offers, and priority access for my patrons on Patreon. If you want monthly poetry chapbooks you can't get anywhere else, plus other books and bonuses, join me on Patreon as a poetry patron. Click the following link for more info on Patreon bonuses:

OrnaRoss.com/Poetry-Patrons

AWARD WINNING INSPIRATIONAL POETRY

Orna Ross: Inspirational Poetry Books

If you like uplifting cadences and brushes with the infinite, treat yourself to more powerful

poetry

from this award-winning Irish poet.

FROM THE INSPIRATIONAL POETRY SERIES

Keepers

A book of motivational poetry that encourages you to do what you love, spurs you to greatness, picks you up when you fail and lets you know that, yes, you can make it.

"Ross's verse is technically brilliant, emotionally beguiling and, at times, startling." (Kaleem Raja, The View from Here)

To get *Keepers*, visit:

OrnaRoss.com/Keepers

Allowing Now

Covering themes like mindfulness, meditation, and self-compassion, *Allowing Now* explores the perceptions of a poet for whom everyday moments are both a treasure and an opportunity for growth.

"Not just a collection of good poetry... [but]... an exercise in wellness" (Amazon Review)

To get *Allowing Now*, visit:

OrnaRoss.com/AllowingNow

FROM THE 12 POEMS TO INSPIRE SERIES

Bright Star

An illustrated book of poems about births and beginnings. A beautiful gift for Christmas, or for anyone starting anew.

"A lovely, emotional collection, something to treasure." (*The Bookwormery*)

To get *Bright Star*, visit:

OrnaRoss.com/BrightStar

Night Light As It Rises

This illustrated, inspirational gift book explores grief, consolation, and carrying on. A thoughtful gift for hard times.

"Since my mum died I make sure to take time for honouring her and this spoke to that feeling…" (*Cozy Chapters*)

To get *Night Light as It Rises*, visit:
OrnaRoss.com/NightlightAsItRises

Circle of Life

An illustrated gift book of inspirational poems about mothering–a gift for Mother's Day, or anytime, for anyone who gives care.

To get *Circle of Life*, visit:
OrnaRoss.com/CircleOfLife

ACKNOWLEDGMENTS

My thanks to Jane Dixon-Smith for cover design of this book and the *12 Poems to Inspire* series. To the #IndiePoetryPlease community on Instagram, thank you for reading, thank you for writing. To the publishing team: Sarah Begley, Kayleigh Brindley and Dan Parsons, who get the words from me to the readers. To Philip Lynch, first reader and sometime muse. And a special thanks to my patrons on Patreon, who keep the poems coming. With a bow, thank you all. *Sonas libh go léir.*

x Orna

ABOUT THE POET

Orna Ross is an award-winning and bestselling novelist and poet. She writes historical fiction and inspirational poetry and is a founder-director of the Alliance of Independent Authors (ALLi). Born and raised in Wexford, in the south-east corner of Ireland, she now lives and works in London and St Leonard's-on-Sea, in the south-east corner of England.

Find out more at
OrnaRoss.com

amazon.com/author/OrnaRoss
goodreads.com/ornaross
patreon.com/OrnaRoss

www.ingramcontent.com/pod-product-compliance
Lightning Source LLC
Chambersburg PA
CBHW030311100526
44590CB00012B/591